HER EPIC ADVENTURE

25 DARING WOMEN WHO INSPIRE A LIFE LESS ORDINARY

KIDS
CAN
PRESS

Written by JULIA DE LAURENTIIS JOHNSTON

Illustrated by SALINI PERERA

Contents

WATER........................ 46

*Women who challenged what's possible
on the ocean deep!*

LAND...................... 36

*Women who ventured through earthly extremes,
from dense jungle to searing savanna!*

Imagine a great adventurer ...

Is it someone flying solo across the continent, gritting their teeth as they come in for a bumpy landing? Or strapping on scuba gear, ready to plunge deep into the ocean to study fish that light up all by themselves? Maybe it's someone climbing a mountain just to see if they can reach the top. But however you imagine this brave adventurer, is it a woman?

Are you picturing Arunima Sinha? She became the first woman amputee to reach the peak of Mount Everest. Or how about Diana Nyad? On her fifth try, at age 64, she became the first person to swim from Cuba to Florida without a shark tank.

So many women eager to explore the world have been met with raised eyebrows:

"Is that any place for a woman?"
"Why would you want to do THAT?!"
"Don't you want to settle down?"

Meanwhile, men seeking adventure usually aren't even questioned. Because although it may be human nature to crave adventure, women haven't always had the same chances as men to make their dreams come true.

But things are beginning to change, and the fight for gender equality has come a long way. Still, some people, such as transgender women and gender non-conforming people (those who don't identify with any gender), find much of the world an unwelcoming place to achieve their dreams — as adventurers or otherwise. The stories in this book show what people — *all* people — are capable of.

So, if you're thirsting for great adventure, read on and let these women show you how it's done. (*kisses biceps*)

SKY

Look Up, Waaay Up!

Today it's no big deal to see an airplane in the sky. But that wasn't always the case. When the Wright brothers landed their first plane more than 100 years ago in 1903, many saw it as the birth of human flight. For years afterward, few people had the chance to ride in a plane — let alone *fly* one! And, certainly, very few women had those opportunities. But, as always, there were some fierce women pioneers who earned their pilot's license and took to the skies.

As people set their sights even higher — from the sky to outer space — smart, capable women put up their hands to say, "Save that seat for me!" They journeyed to space stations, conducting experiments and uncovering the secrets of the universe. And so, we take a look at women who might have gazed up at the sky and wondered, *What the heck is it like up there?*

BESSIE COLEMAN

1892–1926, United States

The world didn't really want Bessie Coleman to succeed. Born in Texas in 1892, she lived in a time and place where it was uncommon for Black and Native American women like her to hold positions of power. In fact, as the child of farm workers, Bessie was often told that her only career option was to be a domestic worker. But she had other ideas. Bessie wanted to be a pilot.

TO THE SKIES

After being rejected by every flight school in the country (because she was both a person of color and a woman), Bessie taught herself to speak French so she could earn her pilot's license in France. In 1921 — two years before Amelia Earhart got her license — she became the world's first Black aviatrix. Since commercial flights weren't a thing yet, Bessie became a trick pilot to make a living. She performed aerial stunts for crowds at air shows, loop-the-looping at state fairs to many cries of "Holy cow!" and "Would ya look at that!"

Bessie insisted that all her shows be desegregated, meaning white and Black people would use the same entrance and sit together. This was a big deal back then, especially in the southern United States, where there were many laws that treated Black people like second-class citizens. But show organizers knew Bessie could pack in the crowds, so they did what she asked.

SOARING IN SOLIDARITY

Bessie was a brilliant self-promoter and believed that the way she lived her life set an example of the greatness Black people could achieve. Sometimes she took other Black women up in her plane — women who, like her, had been told they would never amount to much. Bessie wanted them to experience something very few had at the time: the glory and magic of human flight.

Her next dream was to open a flight school for Black people. But tragically, at 34 years old, she was killed in a plane crash before she could make that happen. A few years later, the Bessie Coleman Aero Club was founded in Los Angeles to make aviation accessible to the Black community. Every year on the anniversary of Bessie's death, Black pilots honor her by air-dropping flowers onto her grave.

Tricks of a Trick Pilot

➡ **BARREL ROLL** *Rolling the plane sideways while flying forward to corkscrew through the air. Don't try it after lunch!*

➡ **LOOP THE LOOP** *Pointing the nose of the plane up and back to make a giant circle in the sky. Hold on to your sunglasses!*

➡ **DIVE** *Nose-diving the plane toward the ground at an extreme angle ... and then pulling up at the last minute. Only for those with nerves of steel.*

AMELIA EARHART

↔ ~~~~~~~~~~~~~~~~ ↔

1897–1937, United States

> **ADVENTURE**
> is worthwhile
> in itself.

The story of Amelia Earhart has become larger than life — the fearless pilot who attempted to fly around the world but mysteriously disappeared after taking off from a Pacific island. Some think she vanished into the infamous Bermuda Triangle. Others say she assumed a new identity and lived out the rest of her days on a tropical island. But there's a lot more to Amelia than her famous legend!

MEANT FOR THE SKIES

As a young woman, Amelia saw a World War I fighter pilot performing aerial tricks at an exhibition. The little red airplane nose-dived right toward her, and Amelia was amazed! In 1920, when she got a chance to ride in a plane for the first time, she was sure that life was for her. "I knew I had to fly," she said.

HOPPING OVER THE POND

Amelia earned her pilot's license in 1923 and was soon breaking records. In 1928, she became the first woman passenger to fly across the Atlantic Ocean. (At that time, few people had flown that far!)

By 1932, she decided to attempt the flight alone. She took off from Harbour Grace, Newfoundland, with the goal of landing in Paris, France. But she miscalculated, flying too far north and, after about 15 hours, came to a bumpy landing on some farmland in Derry, Northern Ireland. When a farmer asked, "Have you flown far?" Amelia chuckled and said, "From America!" She had become the first woman to fly solo across the Atlantic.

THE FINAL FLIGHT

A few years later, Amelia wanted to be the first woman to fly around the world. Her Lockheed Electra 10E was tricked out with an oversized fuel tank and an extra engine. On June 1, 1937, Amelia and her navigator took off from Oakland, California. After several fuel stops, they had made it three-quarters of the way around the world. They took off from Papua New Guinea (just north of Australia) on July 2 and later that day sent out their last known transmission from somewhere over the Pacific Ocean. Amelia and her navigator were never heard from again. But to this day, her name is synonymous with the idea of an intrepid adventurer.

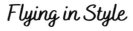

Flying in Style

In the 1930s, pilots sure dressed differently than they do today! The cockpits of those early planes were exposed to the open air — and boy, could it get chilly up there, since the air high in the sky is way colder than at ground level. So, it was important to dress warmly while flying. Here are some things those old-timey pilots might have worn:

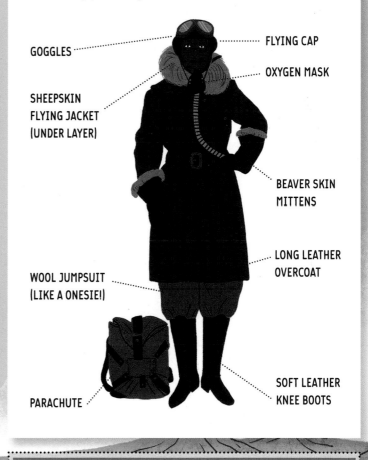

GOGGLES

SHEEPSKIN FLYING JACKET (UNDER LAYER)

WOOL JUMPSUIT (LIKE A ONESIE!)

PARACHUTE

FLYING CAP

OXYGEN MASK

BEAVER SKIN MITTENS

LONG LEATHER OVERCOAT

SOFT LEATHER KNEE BOOTS

← ∼∼∼∼∼ Did You Know? ∼∼∼∼∼ →

Some people think Amelia disappeared while flying over the Bermuda Triangle, but that's in the Atlantic Ocean, halfway around the world from her last transmitted signal. So much for that theory!

Many people don't see a connection between science and dance, but I consider them both to be expressions of the **BOUNDLESS CREATIVITY** that people have to share with one another.

MAE JEMISON

Born 1956, United States

When Mae Jemison was growing up in Chicago in the 1960s, she just had a feeling she would go to space one day. By the time she was a teenager, and people had actually walked on the moon, she was *certain* she, too, would become an astronaut. She figured that when she was a grown-up, people would be going to space the way they went to work — like, *all the time*. No big deal.

TO DANCE OR TO DOCTOR?

Even though Mae had always wanted to be an astronaut, she thought other jobs might be fun, too. When her kindergarten teacher asked Mae what she wanted to be when she grew up, she said, "A scientist!" *Or maybe a doctor,* she thought. But she also had all kinds of hobbies — above all, she loved to dance. Mae struggled to decide whether she wanted to study dance or medicine until her mother gave her this advice: "Well, you can always be a doctor who dances, but it's much harder to be a dancer who doctors!"

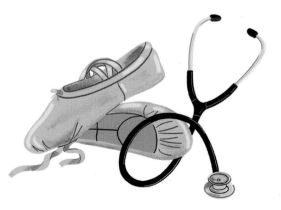

And so, Mae graduated from medical school in 1981. She then entered the Peace Corps, serving as a medical officer in Sierra Leone and Liberia. But soon, she wondered about what else she might do with her career … and her life. Mae hadn't forgotten about her long-held dream to go to space.

NEXT STOP, THE STARS

Mae decided to apply to NASA's astronaut training program and was chosen out of 2000 candidates. In 1992, as a crew member of Space Shuttle *Endeavour,* she became the first Black woman in space.

While on the *Endeavour,* Mae studied the effects of weightlessness and motion sickness on her fellow crew members as they orbited Earth. She took note of their symptoms, such as lack of appetite and "space fog" (which is not the weather forecast, but rather when a person has trouble concentrating or staying alert at such high altitudes). Thanks to Mae's experiments, scientists now better understand how the human body reacts in space and how astronauts can stay healthy while they're up there.

Turn to page 8 to read more about Bessie Coleman!

← ~~~ Did You Know? ~~~ →

Mae brought a photo of Bessie Coleman, the first Black woman pilot, with her to space.

Your Body in Space

Traveling in space can be rough on the human body. Here are a few things that might happen when you're living the gravity-free life:

➡ **WEAK BODY** Without gravity, your skeleton and muscles don't have to work as hard to keep you upright and moving around. Your bone mass decreases, resulting in weaker bones, and your muscles also weaken and get sore from lack of use.

➡ **MOON FACE** Your body is about 60 percent water, most of it found in your veins and at the microscopic cell level. The lack of gravity in space forces fluid to your upper half, giving you a thick, veiny neck, congested sinuses and a puffy face. The effect is fittingly nicknamed "moon face."

➡ **LOSS OF APPETITE** Motion sickness can make it hard to keep anything down — especially those freeze-dried, vacuum-packed meals that are on the menu.

PEAKS

On Top of the World

For thousands of years, people have been in awe of mountains. But it wasn't until the late 1800s that mountaineering became a formal sport. Like many sports at the time, mountain climbing was considered too tough for women. Famed British mountaineer Albert Mummery described three levels of difficulty: an inaccessible peak, the most difficult ascent in the Alps or "an easy day for a lady." He figured that if a woman could climb a particular mountain, it wasn't that hard to climb. (Eye-roll emoji.)

Sure enough, there were women who would prove Albert wrong. They climbed the world's highest peaks, ventured into lava-spewing volcanoes and challenged the perception of what a woman can do!

To me, [climbing] is the most **WONDERFUL** feeling a woman could have.

JIMENA LIDIA HUAYLLAS

Born 1968, Bolivia

Jimena Lidia Huayllas and her friends were very familiar with the high mountains surrounding their beloved city of La Paz, Bolivia. They worked as cooks at the mountaineers' base camps, where they would hear daring tales of climbers scaling soaring peaks. Jimena and her friends longed to hike to those heights, too, and experience what it felt like to be on top of the world. So she asked her friends, "If others can do it, why not us?"

DON'T DRINK THE HATERADE

Jimena's kids thought it was a bad idea for her to climb mountains. They worried that she or her friends might get hurt. After all, the women had no formal climbing training and some were in their 50s. Some people also told them that mountain climbing wasn't for women. "How can you climb up a mountain? That's wrong," they were told. Their culture had traditional beliefs about what a woman could — and *couldn't* — do. But these women didn't listen to the worries or criticism. They still wanted to share this challenge, and victory, with one another and knew they could do it.

THE CHOLITAS CLIMBERS

In 2015, the crew of 10 women climbed their first mountain. But they dressed differently from your average mountaineer. Known as Cholitas, these Aymara Indigenous women wore full colorful skirts, shawls, woven shoes, bowler hats and dangly earrings. Their traditional Cholita clothing was important to their identity, even when scaling icy peaks. Their only compromises were for safety: switching out their woven shoes for hiking boots and crampons, and their bowler hats for helmets.

Their distinctive style sent their critics a strong message: "Not only are we proud Cholitas, but don't tell us what we can and cannot do!" Naturally, they called themselves the Cholitas Climbers.

Now that some of the Cholitas have achieved their goal of climbing the highest peaks of South America, they've set their sights even higher: Mount Everest!

A Mountain Climber's Gear

Here is some essential equipment you'll need to be a mountaineer like the Cholitas Climbers:

➡ **CRAMPONS** These spiky claws attached to the bottom of your hiking boots give your feet a good grip on slippery ice and rock.

➡ **HELMET** When you climb at such heights, a helmet is necessary protection in case you fall. It can also save your noggin from falling rocks, ice and other debris.

➡ **ICE AX** This handheld ax has a spike on the bottom and an ice pick on the top. It can be used as a walking stick, to cut a footpath on slippery ice or to help you brake if you start sliding down a slope.

> A leg is obviously required to climb Mount Everest, but what is needed most is **A BRAVE HEART**.

ARUNIMA SINHA

Born 1988, India

In 2011, Arunima Sinha was traveling on a train headed for Delhi, India. The 24-year-old may have been thinking about volleyball — she had competed at the national level in India. She was approached by some men, who demanded she hand over a gold chain she was wearing. Not one to be easily intimidated, Arunima refused. There was a fight, and the men threw her from the moving train. She survived the fall, but an oncoming locomotive ran over her left leg. It had to be amputated below the knee.

HER STORY TO TELL

Recovering in the hospital, Arunima felt weak and vulnerable. *Who will marry her now?* visitors wondered. There were even upsetting rumors that she had jumped from the train to avoid the ticket collector or even to kill herself. Arunima wanted to take back her story, and her life, and resolved to do something to show people how strong she was. She decided to climb Mount Everest.

TO THE TOP!

Arunima was fitted with a prosthetic leg, which can take months — or even years — to get used to. But not for Arunima. She was walking within two days! She contacted Bachendri Pal, who had been the first Indian woman, in 1984, to climb Mount Everest. Bachendri agreed to train Arunima for the grueling climb.

After 18 months of rigorous training and a mountaineering class, Arunima felt as ready as she was going to be. Climbing the tallest mountain in the world was already going to be a challenge, but a few unexpected challenges popped up, too. Her local guide almost refused to accompany her to the top, believing success was impossible with Arunima's prosthetic leg. It's true she needed more time than most climbers — the ankle and heel of her prosthetic would swivel and often cause her to lose her grip on the icy slopes. But Arunima knew that she wasn't any less capable — she just needed to climb at her own pace.

On May 21, 2013, she reached the summit of Everest after a 52-day journey. She became the first woman amputee to climb the highest peak in the world.

THIS WAY TO EVEREST

An Expert's Tips for Climbing with a Prosthetic

Mountain climbing with a prosthetic comes with its own unique challenges. Here are some pointers from the experts for doing it right:

➡ **TALK IT OVER** *As with any demanding undertaking, communication is key. Before you go, talk to fellow climbers about expectations, particular challenges or anything else that will help make the climb a success!*

➡ **PRACTICE CLIMBS** *Go on a few long practice climbs to pinpoint any possible areas of pain and to consider what pain relievers might be useful for the actual climb.*

➡ **EXTRA PARTS** *Bring spare parts and simple tools to repair a prosthetic that gets damaged along the way. Duct tape can also be handy in a pinch!*

➡ **ONE STEP AT A TIME** *Move at a pace that feels safe and comfortable — this goes for climbers of any ability!*

ICE

Destination: Chillsville

A hundred years ago, most polar expeditions would not accept women adventurers. The leaders, who were always men, thought women were too delicate and weak to endure the harsh conditions. Still, when a British Antarctic expedition was proposed in 1937, 1300 women applied … and they were *all* denied.

Fortunately, things have changed a lot since then, and many intrepid women have braved the world's harshest and most unforgiving climates. They've faced the unimaginable cold of the frozen tundra — winter at the North Pole drops to a chilling -40°C (-40°F); at the South Pole, the temperature reaches -60°C (-76°F). In the Arctic, they've fended off fierce polar bears. (They're not always cute and cuddly in real life!) And in Antarctica, they've dealt with extreme isolation since no one lives there permanently. After a few months, even the most dedicated adventurers get sick of living in an outdoor freezer. Are you ready to meet some of these amazing groundbreakers (or, should we say, icebreakers)?

ADA BLACKJACK

1898–1983, United States

Ada Blackjack didn't choose to be an adventurer to chase a lifelong dream. She did it for her family. Ada was an Iñupiat woman raised in Alaska. Two of her three children had died when they were young, and her surviving son, Bennett, had tuberculosis. His medicine was expensive, and the money Ada made from working odd jobs was running out. Heartbroken, Ada had to place Bennett in an orphanage. Then, she applied to be a seamstress on an Arctic expedition — the money was just too good to pass up. She would join four men, and a cat named Vic, as they colonized Wrangel Island — an expanse of ice west of Alaska in the Arctic Ocean. She hoped to earn enough from the expedition to afford Bennett's medicine and be reunited with him.

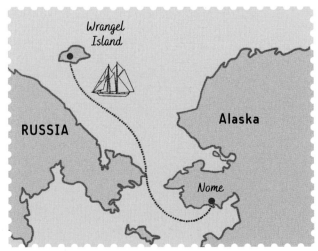

28

LEARNING TO SURVIVE

In 1921, the crew set out aboard the *Silver Wave*. The ship left them on Wrangel Island and was meant to return in one year. But their ride home never arrived, and the crew was stranded on the island. Their provisions ran out after they grossly miscalculated their ability to survive off the land. After many difficult months, with no sign of rescue, all four men were dead. Ada was left with only Vic the cat for company.

Raised by missionaries, Ada didn't posses much Traditional Iñupiat Knowledge and so, impressively, had to learn how to survive the harsh climate all on her own. She figured out how to trap animals for food, how to build a lookout platform to track predatory polar bears and how to shoot a gun. And then, miraculously, in late summer 1923, Ada was rescued by a passing ship. She had survived alone on the remote island for two whole months!

A RELUCTANT HEROINE

Ada returned to Alaska to a lot of praise and the papers calling her a "female Robinson Crusoe." All the attention made her uncomfortable. What Ada wanted most was to retrieve Bennett from the orphanage and pay for his medicine. Happily, she did and was able to watch her son grow up.

Tips for Surviving in the Arctic

If you find yourself at the top of the world (literally!), these tips will help you survive:

➼ **WATCH THE ICE** *White ice is the safest to travel on since it's the thickest, usually 15–30 cm (6–12 in.). Gray ice is considered "young ice" and is only 10–15 cm (4–6 in.) thick. It may support your weight but avoid it if you can. Black ice is usually newly formed and thin, and you'll probably fall through. Avoid it at all costs!*

➼ **DETER POLAR BEARS** *Polar bears can't see very well and are scared by loud noises. Arctic trekkers often carry bear bangers — loud, flashy flares. Before these polar bear firecrackers existed, most Arctic explorers traveled with dogs. Dogs can sense when bears are nearby, and their loud barking can help scare the predators away.*

➼ **EAT A LOT** *A day in the Arctic requires you to consume wayyy more calories than usual. A full day of snowmobile travel can burn 3350 calories. (That's 1.5 times more than the average adult burns in an entire day!) So bring your favorite high-calorie foods! Chocolate bar, anyone?*

IN-YOUNG AHN

Born 1954, South Korea

Antarctic exploration is a pretty tough gig, to say the least. Never-ending ice and cold. Isolation. And then there's the darkness. From mid-May until August, the sun doesn't rise in the South Pole — talk about a long night! But scientist In-Young Ahn was too drawn to Antarctic exploration to be discouraged by any of this. She wanted to study Antarctic marine life, even if it meant conducting experiments in the dark! She packed all her woollies and science equipment and got herself ready to live that #antarcticlife.

PUTTING THE "ICE" IN "ISOLATION"

When In-Young arrived in Antarctica in 1991, she was the first South Korean woman ever to set foot on the "white continent." She was also the only woman scientist at any of the research stations that summer. (Antarctic exploration mainly takes place during the continent's summer months, roughly November to March, when the days are longer and warmer, and there's less snow.)

Being the only woman at the research station had its challenges. The facility wasn't built to include women — for example, there was no women's shower! So the communal shower room was cleared out at a specific time each day for In-Young to bathe. And sometimes In-Young felt pretty lonely without any other women to relate to.

TOO CURIOUS TO QUIT

Even with its challenges, In-Young returned to explore Antarctica each summer. She conducted important research about the Antarctic clam and the impact of glacier retreat on the coast. Her studies have mainly helped us to understand how climate change is affecting the wildlife on Antarctica's icy shore.

In 2015, In-Young became the first Asian woman to become an Antarctic station leader, overseeing the team of researchers at the Korean Antarctic Station. And it just might be thanks to her willingness to take those first snowy steps that today she isn't the only woman scientist trekking around the icy continent: now about one-third of Antarctic scientists are women.

Did You Know?

Antarctica has 70 research stations where scientists live and work. They're operated by 29 different countries. That's why Antarctica is sometimes known as the "international continent." It's a place of worldwide cooperation in the name of science.

What Happens at an Antarctic Research Center?

Antarctica has a unique environment that is mostly untouched by humans. Scientists can do experiments there that can't be done anywhere else in the world. So what exactly are they researching down there?

➡ **WILDLIFE** During the Antarctic summer, there's wildlife everywhere to observe and study. Penguins, albatross and other seabirds come ashore to lay their eggs and raise their young. Marine mammals such as humpback whales and Antarctic fur seals stay close to the shore while searching for krill to feed on.

➡ **CLIMATE CHANGE** Scientists can measure climate change by looking at Antarctica's ice. They drill into the ground and extract long ice tubes called ice cores. These tubes show layers of snow and ice that act as a record and provide clues about the planet's changing conditions. It's sort of like how the rings of a tree can tell you its story, too.

KAREN DARKE

Born 1971, England

Karen Darke felt like she was born with the adventure gene — she had always loved skiing, mountain biking and rock climbing. At 21 years old, she was climbing the cliffs of Aberdeen, Scotland, when she slipped and fell onto the jagged rocks below. The accident left her paralyzed from the chest down. Karen was devastated when doctors told her she would never walk again. Were her adventuring days behind her?

ROAD TO RECOVERY

Following her accident, Karen spent six months in the hospital. She had a lot of time to think about her life ahead. Was her body still capable of doing the activities she loved so much? Once her injuries started to heal and she got stronger, Karen decided to take up wheelchair racing. And just a little more than a year after her fall, she crossed the finish line of the London Marathon!

PUSHING FORWARD

One of Karen's greatest adventures was in 2006 on a month-long expedition in Greenland. She skied across 600 km (373 mi.) of frozen tundra along with a few fellow expeditioners. Sitting on her specially designed skis, she used ski poles to propel herself forward, traveling through the blinding, biting wind and snow.

Karen knew the icy journey would be hard, but she faced some particular challenges because of her disability. The paralyzed parts of her body couldn't recognize the signs that she was cold, such as chills or numbness, and relay that information to her brain. So Karen had to closely monitor her internal temperature and regulate it by layering her clothing. And gripping the ski poles to push herself forward was so hard on her hands that some days she couldn't uncurl her fingers because the tendons were so tight.

Since the Greenland expedition, Karen has continued to find extraordinary ways to challenge herself. She became a Paralympian in handcycling and has even climbed El Capitan — a popular spot for rock climbers in California's Yosemite National Park. That climb required her to do more than 4000 pull-ups to get to the top!

How Does a Paralympian Train?

The Paralympic Games is an international sporting event for athletes living with a variety of disabilities. Paralympians adjust their training based on the kind of disability they live with — an athlete who has a visual impairment may need to train differently than someone like Karen, who has impaired muscular power. But whatever the sport or the ability, all elite athletes have a few things in common when training for a big event.

➡ **HITTING THE GYM** *Performing a sport at a competitive level requires tip-top strength and endurance, and that means serious training most days.*

➡ **EATING RIGHT** *An athelete's body is like a machine, fueled by the right food combos for vitamins and nutrients. And, no, cheeseburger combos don't count!*

➡ **KNOWING LIMITS** *Athletes often push themselves to their physical limits, but they also know when to back down to avoid injury.*

➡ **GETTING REST** *Training puts a huge demand on the muscles, and sleep is how the body repairs itself. In other words, you snooze not to lose!*

> When on expedition, we are putting ourselves into dangerous environments. I take many safety precautions, but there is **ALWAYS A RISK**.

SARAH MCNAIR-LANDRY

Born 1986, Canada

Arctic exploring runs in Sarah McNair-Landry's family. Her parents are legendary Arctic adventurers, and her mom, Matty, led the first all-women expedition to the North Pole in 1997. Growing up on Baffin Island, Nunavut, Sarah also felt quite at home on the ice: skating, skiing and dogsledding. Soon she began to wonder about all the other icy landscapes in the world waiting to be explored. But she didn't just want to see pictures of them or hear stories about them — she wanted to experience them for herself.

A POLAR RECORD

At the age of 18, Sarah's desire for icy adventure took her on an expedition down south — like, as far south as you can go. She skied unsupported (meaning all human powered, without motorized vehicles or other help) from the coast of Antarctica to the South Pole — a 3000 km (1864 mi.) journey. A year later, she hopped on a dogsled to venture to the North Pole and became the youngest person to reach both poles.

HITTING THE ICE

Though she's crossed the Greenland ice sheet six times, there's one trip Sarah definitely won't forget. In 2016, she and two friends decided to trek 966 km (600 mi.) across Greenland to a wild Arctic river and then kayak down the rapids. On their way, Sarah was kite skiing when a strong gust of wind jerked her skyward. She was pulled 6 m (20 ft.) into the air and then dropped onto the hard, unforgiving ice. Sarah's helmet cracked, and she was knocked unconscious.

Sarah woke up sore. (An X-ray later revealed a cracked vertebra. *Ouch!*) Most people would have gone home after an injury like that. But Sarah was the only one who knew the team's planned route through the icy crevasses and glaciers. She wanted to keep going. After five days of rest, Sarah started kite skiing again since it was the quickest way to get to the river. Eventually, the team arrived at their destination and kayaked, victorious and exhausted, down the river. They even plunged down the river's three massive waterfalls — adventurers till the very end!

Surfing on Ice

Kite skiing is sort of like kitesurfing, but on snow and ice. The kite is harnessed to the skier's waist. When a gust of wind comes along, the kite propels the skier over the ice. With good winds, an experienced kite skier can travel up to 100 km/h (62 mph)! Kite skiers always wear a helmet to help them stay safe when traveling at such speeds.

Born to Be Wild

Throughout history, hiking off the beaten path has been a dangerous adventure. While some feared getting mauled by a bear, eaten by a jaguar or swallowed by an anaconda, it was often the not-so-scary things that they really needed to watch out for. An expedition could come to a quick (and sometimes fatal!) end after tripping on an unseen vine and breaking a bone, having a deadly reaction to a plant or getting dangerously dehydrated. That's a lot to worry about — including, you know, getting mauled by a bear, eaten by a jaguar or swallowed by an anaconda.

Many fearless women, however, were born to live on the wild side. You'll read about those who ventured into jungles, through dense forests or across sweeping savannas. Being an adventurer like them requires the right gear, proper training, strong survival skills and lots of gumption. And two other words of advice? Bug spray.

CHARLOTTE SMALL

1785–1857, Turtle Island
(Indigenous name for North America)

Charlotte Small was born in Sakitawak (the Nehiyaw name for Île-à-la-Crosse, Saskatchewan) at the height of the fur trade. Charlotte had a Scottish father, who left the family when she was a child, and a Nehiyaw (or Cree) mother, who raised Charlotte and her siblings in the Nehiyaw tradition.

Turtle Island was being taken over by white European settlers who were stealing the land from the Indigenous Peoples who had lived there for generations. These settlers wanted to profit from the land's resources. But to venture across the unfamiliar landscape, they often relied on Indigenous women as guides who knew how to survive in often unforgiving conditions.

ON THE MOVE

When Charlotte was 13, she became a "country wife," the term that settlers used to refer to the Indigenous women they married. She wed 29-year-old David Thompson, a fur trader, explorer and mapmaker from England. (At the time, it wasn't uncommon for teenage girls to marry adult men.) Together they traveled through large parts of Turtle Island: endless thick forests, long winding rivers and the great expanse of the Rocky Mountains. They were some of the first people to put what is now known as Western Canada on the map — literally. Using the information gathered during their years of exploration, David drew maps of almost *half* of North America.

SURVIVAL SKILLS

Without Charlotte's Traditional Knowledge, experience of the terrain and language skills, she and her family wouldn't have been able to survive these often perilous expeditions. In fact, sometimes her hunting skills were what kept them from starving. With their young children in tow (they would eventually have 13 in total!), Charlotte and her husband traveled 40 000 km (24 854 mi.) across the country — by foot, on horseback or in a canoe. That's 3.5 times farther than famed American explorers Lewis and Clark! (In many history books, it's David alone who gets all the glory. But *we* know better!)

"Hello, Bonjour, Tân'si!"

As well as being resourceful and resilient, Charlotte was also a skilled translator. She was fluent in Cree, English and French and familiar with several other Indigenous languages. On their travels, their team would have encountered both Indigenous Peoples and Europeans. To say hello, she might have said "Tân'si" (TAN-say) in Cree or "Bonjour!" (bon-JOOR) in French.

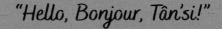

ZORA NEALE HURSTON

1891–1960, United States

Zora Neale Hurston was a celebrated writer who could shape feelings into beautiful turns of phrase and create vivid descriptions. She is most famous for her major role in the Harlem Renaissance, an intellectual and artistic movement named for a mostly Black neighborhood in 1920s New York. But Zora was also an anthropologist who studied how human societies and cultures develop. She was especially interested in Black cultures and identities in the Americas. And so, in 1936, Zora traveled to Haiti, and later to Jamaica, to study up close a religion that she felt was often misunderstood: voodoo.

INTO THE JUNGLE

Zora was one of the first American anthropologists allowed access to everyday life in the Caribbean. While in Haiti, she was even invited on a five-day boar hunt through the jungle — not something usually offered to outsiders! But it was voodoo she was most curious about. Zora immersed herself in as many firsthand experiences with the religion as she possibly could.

Much of voodoo focuses on the healing powers of herbs and plants. Trekking through the thick brush of the Haitian jungle, Zora learned how to spot and harvest many voodoo ingredients, such as the Jatropha plant (handy for releasing the trapped souls of the dead or getting rid of evil spirits). She even came face-to-face with someone who locals believed to be a zombie.

A RIPPLE EFFECT

When she returned home, Zora shared her fieldwork and research with other academics. Few people at the time were studying African-American culture like she was. Zora also wrote a book, *Tell My Horse*, detailing her experiences on the islands. It included many things she learned about voodoo. Zora's deep dive into a subject few had thought worthy had a ripple effect. Others across the United States and beyond began seriously studying different aspects of African-American culture.

What Is Vodou*?

When enslaved West and Central African people were brought to the New World, they were forbidden from practicing their religions. So they hid their spiritual practices from the slave owners by using elements of Catholicism (for example, disguising spirits as saints). The result was vodou, a blend of these religions.

Some people think vodou is all about sticking pins into a doll that looks like someone you don't like! But in reality, the religion has a pretty positive outlook. For example, women known as Vodou Queens or Priestesses lead rituals to summon spirits for healing, love and prosperity. Amulets, also known as gris-gris or mojo bags, usually contain small objects or dried herbs that are blessed. They're worn to manifest such things as fertility, confidence and good luck.

*People who practice the religion today prefer this spelling.

> Anywhere there's a crack of dirt in the sidewalk, a medicinal plant will **GROW**.

ROSITA ARVIGO

Born 1941, United States

Rosita Arvigo believed nature had something to teach her. Born to Iranian and Italian parents, she grew up in Chicago, Illinois. But city life was not for her, so in 1969 she moved to a farm in Mexico. There, Rosita learned about nature's growing seasons, such as knowing that delicious mangoes grow in July. And traditional healers taught her how to use plants for medicine. She discovered how to soothe a headache with a mix of *chalalatli* root and tobacco. *In what other ways*, she wondered, *could the natural gifts of the earth be used?*

MEETING DESTINY

Eventually, Rosita moved to Belize, where she met Don Elijio Panti, an almost 90-year-old Maya healer. Where most would see plants and leaves, he saw the ingredients for medicine. This knowledge came from the ancient Maya civilization and had been handed down from teacher to apprentice for thousands of years.

HEADACHE HELPER

Don Elijio told Rosita that no one wanted to learn about these traditional ways anymore. Sure, some people were interested in learning just enough to cure a headache or ease sore muscles. But it would take years of studying to learn everything that Don Elijio knew. He was like a walking encyclopedia! Suddenly, Rosita's destiny seemed clear: she would become Don Elijio's apprentice. Thankfully, after a year of proving herself to Don Elijio, he agreed.

THE PEOPLE'S PHARMACY

Far from the urban world of her youth, Rosita spent the next 12 years trekking the rainforests of Belize every week with Don Elijio, swatting away buzzing bugs and stomping through the sticky mud. She learned how to categorize the rainforest's plants, roots and leaves and how to transform them into salves, potions and tinctures for healing. And understanding that a wealth of ancient education could be lost, she carefully recorded all she learned in a book. To Rosita, the rainforest was the People's Pharmacy — a place to find everything you needed to feel better.

A Healer's Medicine Cabinet*

Instead of going to a pharmacy, Maya healers gather and prepare their medicines from the earth. Here are some things they might have on hand:

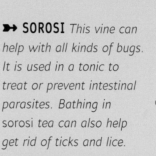

➼ **CONTRIBO** *This plant smells like rotting meat. (Ew!) But it helps battle the common cold and eases digestion. (Phew!)*

➼ **SOROSI** *This vine can help with all kinds of bugs. It is used in a tonic to treat or prevent intestinal parasites. Bathing in sorosi tea can also help get rid of ticks and lice.*

➼ **GAUZUMA ULMIFOLIA** *Slip a slice of bark from this type of cedar tree into your boots to battle stinky feet — and it'll even get rid of your foot fungus.*

➼ **IXCANAN** *This plant, named for the Maya Goddess of the Forest and Healing, can cure many skin ailments, such as insect bites, rashes, burns and sores.*

*Disclaimer: Not to be tried at home, except maybe if you have 12 years of training like Rosita!

THE BLACK MAMBAS

Founded 2013, South Africa

The Balule Nature Reserve is a wildlife conservation area in South Africa teeming with wild animals, such as lions, elephants, buffalo, leopards and rhinoceroses. Unfortunately, bushmeat hunters and poachers hunt these animals and sell their meat, tusks or horns. Luckily for the animals — and *not* so luckily for the illegal hunters — there are the Black Mambas. This group of more than 30 local women is specially trained to look after the reserve and help protect the animals.

> I want to **PROTECT NATURE** and make sure that my children and future generations can see rhinos and all other wildlife, not just [as] pictures in books.

DON'T MESS WITH THE MAMBAS

The Black Mambas are the world's first anti-poaching unit made up almost entirely of women. They patrol the reserve to keep the bushmeat hunters and poachers outta there. They monitor the wildlife area by looking for human tracks, sounds of gunshots or any other suspicious activity. During their patrols, they conduct roadblocks and release animals from snares set by poachers. The Black Mambas even keep watch in the dark of night. Whenever they find anything out of the ordinary, they call for backup and do all they can to fend off anyone who would hurt or disturb the animals.

HEROES IN CAMO

The Black Mambas go through paramilitary-style training (a sort of military boot camp) to help get them ready to survey and protect the reserve. They don't carry guns — the Mambas take a non-violent approach to anti-poaching, instead using their presence in the park as their most powerful weapon against illegal activities. But being unarmed means things can get a bit hairy when, say, a patrol finds itself surrounded by lions, which did happen once! (Fortunately, a local landowner happened by and chased the animals away.)

When the unit was first formed, many men in the community doubted that women could do the job. But the Black Mambas sure have changed some minds. Since they started patrolling the reserve, incidents of poaching have gone down by more than 70 percent! And the Black Mambas are also having an impact outside the reserve's boundaries — they're teaching local schoolchildren how to be the next generation of wildlife conservationists.

Some heroes may wear capes, but the Black Mambas prefer their camo!

A Walk on the Wild Side

When you're a member of the Black Mambas, the expression "a walk in the park" has a special meaning. Here are just some of the wild animals the Mambas might encounter on their patrols:

➤➤ **LIONS** *These fierce, wild cats are often the prey of poachers looking to sell their bones, which are ground up and used in traditional medicines.*

➤➤ **RHINOS** *The rising demand for rhino horn, believed to have healing properties in traditional medicines, has resulted in the dwindling numbers of these powerful animals.*

➤➤ **PANGOLINS** *Each year, more than 20 000 pangolins (known as "scaly anteaters") are sold on the black market for their meat, considered a delicacy in some countries, and for their scales, used in traditional medicines.*

Making Waves

Long ago, male sailors told tales about encounters with mermaids — the only "women" they met out at sea. (They were probably hallucinating from a lack of fresh veggies during those extra-long voyages!) But unbeknownst to those sailors, some of their fellow seafarers weren't fellas! History tells us that many women dressed in men's clothing so they could sail the high seas, too.

Of course, aquatic adventures are for everyone. And there are so many possibilities on a planet that is more than 70 percent water. Deep-sea diving, open-ocean swimming, big-wave surfing and around-the-world sailing — the women in this section have had some extreme adventures! They also had amazing physical and mental strength to keep their wits about them. Cuz, you know, no one wants to be shark bait.

SYLVIA EARLE

Born 1935, United States

In the 1950s, Sylvia Earle was studying for her science degree. She applied for a job as a teaching assistant, but a man was hired instead. The faculty had figured that Sylvia would probably get married and have kids soon, so they needed to save the sweet jobs for men who might "make use of their education." *(Ugh.)* Plus, at the time, many people thought a woman went to university just to find a smart husband. Not because, you know, she might actually want to *learn something*. Sylvia went on to finish her degree and then earned a PhD in phycology (the study of algae). Over time, she became one of the world's most accomplished oceanographers. She also became a wife and mother. Because women can be whatever they want.

TEAM AQUANAUT!

In 1970, Sylvia led an all-women team of aquanauts (basically, water astronauts) as part of the Tektite II experiment. For two weeks, the team of four lived in an underwater laboratory off the coast of the United States Virgin Islands, where they conducted experiments. They swam day and night, observing and photographing their deep-sea surroundings and witnessing how pollution was changing coral reefs. During this expedition, Sylvia and her team discovered 26 new underwater plants!

TEKTITE II

HER DEEPNESS

After the Tektite II project, Sylvia took part in many other exciting expeditions. In 1979, she made a deep dive in a JIM suit, which looks like an astronaut's space suit, to the ocean floor. At 381 m (1250 ft.) below the water's surface, she undid her safety belt and walked around for two hours. Sylvia saw things no person had ever seen before, such as small sharks with bright green eyes and a forest of corals that looked like giant bed springs. At the time, it was the deepest untethered dive that had ever been done.

Sylvia has spent more than 7000 hours underwater exploring the great mysteries and wonders of the ocean deep. Known affectionately as "Her Deepness" for her royal-like status in the marine biology world, she is a passionate champion for the protection of our world's oceans.

Tips for Deep-Sea Adventuring

Scuba diving can be a dangerous activity, so you need to get proper certification before you try it. But once you do, here are some tips from the pros on how to have a great adventure way down deep:

➼ **BREATHE** You might feel like you can't breathe normally using an oxygen tank. Don't panic! And definitely don't hold your breath! Instead, concentrate on taking regular, steady breaths in and out.

➼ **LOOK UP!** It's easy to be mesmerized by all the wonders in front of you, but don't forget to look up. You might catch a glimpse of bigger sea creatures or a colorful school of fish — they like hanging out closer to the surface.

➼ **FOLLOW THE BUBBLES** Decompression sickness happens when you swim back to the surface too fast. Gas in the body can release too quickly, sort of like opening a bottle of soda pop after shaking it. Try to swim upward at the same pace as the bubbles you breathe out, following them slowly to the surface.

← ~~ Did You Know? ~~ →

Sylvia has been up close and personal with all kinds of dangerous marine life. She once had to kick a shark to avoid being bitten!

DIANA NYAD

Born 1949, United States

Diana Nyad has always felt at home in the water. When she was 25 years old and already an accomplished long-distance swimmer, she decided to swim around the island of Manhattan. On her first try, she caught a virus from the stinky, contaminated water and didn't complete the swim. But she tried again. The 45 km (28 mi.) swim took her nearly eight hours — and got the attention of the *New York Times* and even former First Lady Jackie Kennedy, who called Diana her hero! *If that impressed them*, Diana thought, *they ain't seen nothing yet.*

Never, ever give up. You're never too old to **CHASE YOUR DREAMS.**

ONWARD!

Diana had an even bigger dream: to swim from Havana, Cuba, to Key West, Florida. The shark- and jellyfish-infested waters would take more than two days to cross. At 177 km (110 mi.), it would be the longest open-ocean swim in history ... if she could make it.

Diana attempted the distance four times over 35 years without completing the journey. Something always got in the way, such as a strong wind that knocked her off course or stinging jellyfish (super painful and potentially deadly!). Diana's heart broke a little more each time she didn't reach her goal. Was this a silly idea? Was she wasting her time?

But Diana's girlfriend at the time, Nina, had given her a pendant necklace in the shape of Cuba with the word *onward* engraved on the back — a token that would help give Diana the confidence to keep trying.

IF AT FIRST YOU DON'T SUCCEED ...

In 2013, at the age of 64, Diana made her fifth attempt to swim from Havana to Key West. To keep calm, and help pass the time, she counted and sang songs by The Beatles in her head. When she finally reached Key West, after 53 hours of swimming, Diana became the first person to complete the swim without the aid of a protective shark cage. Moral of the story? If there's something you *reeeally* want to achieve, never give up. (Although if it involves jumping into shark-infested waters, ask your grown-ups first.)

Recipe for Success

What did Diana eat on her epic swim? Every hour and a half, Diana would swim up to the boat that followed close by (without touching it, which would have disqualified her from achieving the world record) and be given a three-course meal:

➼ **APPETIZER** *A drink of water, electrolytes and protein powder (a pre-digested protein so the body can do less work digesting and more work swimming).*

➼ **MAIN COURSE** *A tube of energy gel and chewable cubes containing a balance of nutrients specially made for endurance athletes.*

➼ **DESSERT** *A little bite of banana covered in peanut butter to give her the satisfaction of real food after all those gels, powders and goos!*

←~~ Did You Know? ~~→

Diana's last name means "water nymph" in Greek, which couldn't be more perfect!

MAYA GABEIRA

<-~~~~~~~~~~~~~~~~~~~~~~~~~~~~~->

Born 1987, Brazil

When she was 14 years old, Maya Gabeira would watch her boyfriend and his friends surf the waves off the coast of Rio de Janeiro in Brazil. *I bet I could do that,* she thought. She gave it a try — and realized surfing was a lot harder than it looked! Maya got knocked off her board a lot but soon enough started to get the hang of it. And then, once she mastered regular surfing, she fixed her eye on bigger, badder waves. She began to practice big-wave surfing, cresting on 6 m (20 ft.) waves and then even higher ones. And, as it turns out, Maya was really, really good at it. At age 22, she surfed the biggest wave a woman ever had — a 14 m (46 ft.) wave at Dungeons, a popular spot for big-wave surfing in South Africa.

WIPEOUT!

A few years later, in 2013, Maya set her sights on even bigger waves. She went to Portugal to meet the surf at Nazaré, a place world-famous for its monster "white horses" (that's surfer speak for "waves"). She had trained. She had pumped herself up. She was ready.

Maya hit a rising wave and stood steady on her board. She climbed higher … and higher … and higher until reaching a staggering 24 m (79 ft.). That's about the height of a five-and-a-half story building! It was the biggest, and fastest, wave she had ever ridden. But then … wipeout! Maya was knocked from her board. Tumbling into the ocean, she was trapped in the undertow as four powerful waves crashed over her. Unconscious and with a broken ankle, she nearly drowned before she was rescued.

WAVES OF WILLPOWER

Eventually, Maya recovered from the wipeout. And five years later, in 2018, she returned to Nazaré. She wanted to face her fear and surf at the place that almost killed her. This time, the giant waves wouldn't knock her down. Maya successfully rode a 20.72 m (68 ft.) wave from trough to crest, setting a new Guinness World Record for the largest wave surfed by a woman. In 2020, Maya broke her own world record when she surfed a 22.4 m (73.5 ft.) wave in Nazaré.

Surfer Lingo 101

If you're going to ride the waves, here are some handy surfer phrases to know:

"Look out for the men in gray suits!"

Translation: Look out for sharks!

"Did you see her go through that back door?! Perfect 10!"

Translation: Did you see her enter the curl of the wave from behind it? She rode it perfectly!

"No need to bail. Those are ankle busters!"

Translation: Don't jump off your board. Those waves are too small to ride, anyway!

"She aimed her stick straight for that crest. She was real aggro about it but then wiped out."

Translation: She aimed her surfboard for the top of that wave. She surfed the wave aggressively but then fell off her board.

"I have a few new boards in my quiver, thanks to that tubular shaper."

Translation: I added a few new surfboards to my collection, thanks to that talented surfboard designer.

> As soon as I get on my boat, something inside me changes. Then, I really feel what **LIVING** is.

LAURA DEKKER

Born 1995, New Zealand

You might say that sailing is in Laura Dekker's DNA. Not only was she born on a sailboat, but she also spent the first five years of her life on one, sailing the world with her parents. At an age when most kids were playing in sandboxes, Laura was learning how to navigate the ocean.

SOLO ACT

By the time Laura was 14, she and her family were living in the Netherlands. But life as a landlubber just wasn't for her. Instead, Laura wanted to sail around the world — all by herself. There was just one tiny (okay, not so tiny) problem: the Dutch government said no. A court ruled that Laura was too young to take care of herself on such a long and dangerous journey.

But Laura kept up the fight to make the trip. Finally, a month before her 15th birthday, the courts said it was up to her parents to decide whether she could go. Believing in her, her parents gave Laura permission.

SEEING THE WORLD

Having kept up with her training, Laura was ready to set sail almost immediately. The following month, she launched her trusted 11.5 m (38 ft.) boat, *Guppy,* from a port in Gibraltar, near southern Spain. She sailed across the Atlantic Ocean to the Caribbean island of St. Maarten, which would be her final destination after circumnavigating the globe.

If she could make it, Laura would be the youngest person to sail solo around the world, but she never wanted to be the fastest. She planned to take her time and make extra stops along the way, such as visiting the Galápagos Islands to catch a peek at the blue-footed boobies! But it wasn't all smooth sailing. When Laura hit the rough and windy waters of Cape Point, off the tip of South Africa, she played her flute to help herself stay calm.

Laura's trip around the world took nearly one-and-a-half years (518 days, to be exact!). On January 21, 2012, she arrived back at St. Maarten — marking the finish to her solo sail around the world.

YNES MEXIA

1870–1938, United States

Ynes Mexia became a botanist at the age of 51, when she decided it was time to fulfill her longtime dream to study plants. Over the next 13 years, she adventured through large parts of South and Central America to collect more than 145 000 plants, including 500 new species, 50 of which were named in her honor. She's said to have had a photographic memory, remembering every plant she ever saw!

DERVLA MURPHY

Born 1931, Ireland

After her mother died, 30-year-old Dervla Murphy wanted to do something drastic to help herself heal. So she got on her bicycle (which she called Roz) and rode from Europe to India. Frequently relying on the hospitality of strangers, she traveled alone and with the bare minimum of supplies. She often ran into danger, such as the time she was attacked by wolves in the former Yugoslavia. Dervla continued her adventures around the world well into her 80s and has written more than 20 books, many about her travels.

MARGARET LOWMAN

Born 1953, United States

Margaret Lowman, or "Canopy Meg" as she's known to her pals, was one of the first scientists to study forest canopies (the "roof" created by treetops and overlapping branches). Forest canopies are where most of the world's 30 million species live — in other words, a whole sky-high world! Since no one else had ever spent as much time up there as Canopy Meg, she had to invent ways to explore the treetops. She designed hot-air balloons and special walkway systems to reach those organic laboratories in the sky.

ISABELLE EBERHARDT

1877–1904, Switzerland

Born into an affluent life in Switzerland, Isabelle Eberhardt longed for adventure abroad. But at the time, it wasn't easy for women to travel on their own. So Isabelle dressed in men's clothes — a habit since childhood — and decided to explore the world that way. This adventurer was then able to travel freely throughout North Africa and explore its many cultures and terrains. Isabelle once famously declared, "A nomad I will remain for life, in love with distant and uncharted places."

APARAJITA DATTA

Born 1970, India

Aparajita Datta is an intrepid wildlife biologist who fell in love with hornbills (a type of bird with a distinctive curved beak) while exploring and studying India's Namdapha National Park. When she learned that a local tribal community, the Lisu people, hunted hornbills, she wanted to find a way to protect the animals while respecting the Lisu people's indigenous way of life. With the wisdom of the Lisu hunters, Aparajita helped facilate a community-based conservation program to help improve the quality of life for the Lisu tribe, which had a ripple effect on preserving the park's wildlife.

Interview with an Adventurer
LOIS PRYCE

Born 1973, Scotland

What does it take to be an adventurer today? Why not ask one! Lois Pryce had her first adventure when she was just 13 years old. That's when she and three friends grabbed their bikes and toured around Cornwall, England, for a week — all by themselves! At age 30, she quit her job and hopped on a motorcycle for a 10-month solo journey from Alaska down to Argentina that spanned more than 32 000 km (about 20 000 mi.). Three years later, she did it again, riding 16 000 km (about 10 000 mi.) from London to South Africa. So how does she do it? Let's find out.

You went from working in an office to riding your motorcycle around the world. What made you think you could do it?

I guess I'm an optimist to begin with, and I believed that if someone else has done it, then I could do it, too. I knew that it was technically possible to ride a motorcycle anywhere in the world — so why not me?! I soon realized that if I took it one day at a time, and just kept going, then I would reach my goal. The more I traveled and faced all different kinds of challenges, the more I felt I could overcome.

What surprised you the most about traveling?

I realized that I was more resilient than I thought I was, and I think we all are — we just don't generally find ourselves in situations that test our resilience. Finding myself in potentially difficult situations, I discovered that I was able to draw on reserves of initiative, courage and physical and mental strength that I didn't know I possessed. I was also gratified to learn that the world is a lot more friendly and welcoming than we might think from reading the news or watching television. People are generally good the world over, and the natural instinct is to want to look after a visitor to their country. I received so much unconditional kindness and hospitality from men and women of all nationalities, ages and backgrounds, all over the world.

What advice would you give to someone preparing for an around-the-world adventure?

Bring a good sense of humor, paper maps, a notebook and pen and only two pairs of socks and three pairs of undies. (You can wash them out as you go!) Travel light, take risks, smile a lot, talk to everyone, especially the people who are the most different from you. And, of course, bring a stack of good books to read. (These days, an e-reader has made life a lot easier for traveling bookworms like me!)

What did you learn along the way that you wish you'd known before you left?

That the fears I had before I left were unfounded — I didn't need to worry about all those things that never ended up happening.

Adventuring AROUND the WORLD

The women in this book performed incredible feats around the globe — and beyond! Here are just a few of the locations and routes mentioned in their stories.

1 **Bessie Coleman** became the first Black aviatrix after earning her pilot's license in France (pages 8–9).

2 **Amelia Earhart** flew three-quarters of the way around the world before her mysterious disappearance (pages 10–11).

3 **Mae Jemison** and **Kalpana Chawla** rocketed into space from NASA's launch station in Florida, United States (pages 12–15).

4 **Junko Tabei** was the first woman to climb Mount Everest (pages 18–19). **Arunima Sinha** was the first woman amputee to climb Mount Everest (pages 24–25).

5 **Katia Krafft** predicted the volcanic eruption at Mount Pinatubo in the Philippines, saving many lives (pages 20–21).

6 **Jimena Lidia Huayllas** and the Cholitas Climbers hike the mountains of Bolivia (pages 22–23).

7 **Ada Blackjack** learned how to survive after being deserted on Wrangel Island (pages 28–29).

8 **In-Young Ahn** was the first Asian woman to head an Antarctic research station (pages 30–31).

9 **Karen Darke** traversed Greenland by sit-ski (pages 32–33).

10 **Sarah McNair-Landry** kite skied across Greenland (pages 34–35).

11 **Charlotte Small** explored much of Western Canada with her husband, mapmaker and explorer David Thompson (pages 38–39).

12 **Zora Neale Hurston** studied voodoo in Haiti (pages 40–41).

13 **Rosita Arvigo** learned about traditional medicinal healing in Belize (pages 42–43).

14 **The Black Mambas** protect wild animals on South Africa's Balule Nature Reserve (pages 44–45).

15 **Sylvia Earle** studied marine life from the Tektite II underwater habitat (pages 48–49).

16 **Diana Nyad** swam unaccompanied from Cuba to Florida, United States (pages 50–51).

17 **Maya Gabeira** surfed five-story waves in Portugal (pages 52–53).

18 **Laura Dekker** sailed solo around the world (pages 54–55).

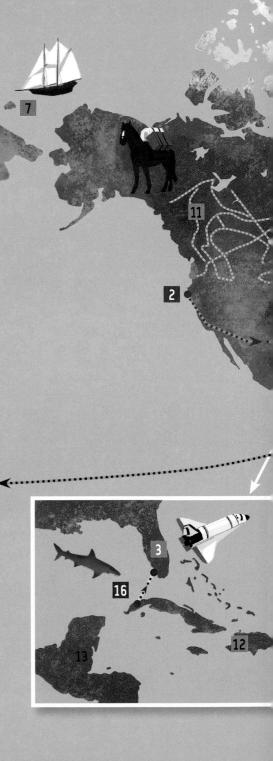

RESOURCES

For Further Exploration
BOOKS

Harrison, Vashti. *Little Leaders: Bold Women in Black History.* New York: Little, Brown Books for Young Readers, 2017.

Maggs, Sam, and Sophia Foster-Dimino. *Wonder Women: 25 Innovators, Inventors, and Trailblazers Who Changed History.* Philadelphia: Quirk Books, 2016.

Ross, Ailsa, and Amy Blackwell. *The Girl Who Rode a Shark: And Other Stories of Daring Women.* Toronto: Pajama Press, 2019.

Skeers, Linda, and Livi Gosling. *Women Who Dared: 52 Fearless Daredevils, Adventurers and Rebels.* Naperville, IL: Sourcebooks, 2017.

Author's Selected Sources
BOOKS

Dekker, Laura. *One Girl One Dream.* New York: HarperCollins Publishers, 2014.

Earle, Sylvia A. *Blue Hope: Exploring and Caring for Earth's Magnificent Ocean.* Washington, DC: National Geographic Society, 2014.

Hurston, Zora Neale. *Tell My Horse: Voodoo and Life in Haiti and Jamaica.* New York, HarperCollins Publishers, [1938] 2008.

Sinha, Arunima. *Born Again on the Mountain: A Story of Losing Everything and Finding It Back.* New York: Penguin Publishing Group, 2014.

Tabei, Junko, and Helen Y. Rolfe. *Honouring High Places: The Mountain Life of Junko Tabei.* Calgary: RMB Rocky Mountain Books, 2017.

ARTICLES

Levy, Ariel. "Breaking the Waves." *New Yorker,* February 3, 2014. https://www.newyorker.com/magazine/2014/02/10/breaking-the-waves. *(An article about Diana Nyad.)*

FILMS

Herzog, Werner, dir. *Into the Inferno.* Matter of Fact Media, Spring Films, Werner Herzog Filmproduktion, 2016.

INDEX

For my parents, for Liam, for the Girls and all their mini-mes but, of course, most especially for Frances — J.D.L.J.

For my mother, Kusum — S.P.

ACKNOWLEDGMENTS: I'd like to acknowledge Wilfred Burton, a Métis author, who worked with us on the profile of Charlotte Small and thank him for his labor and thoughtful insights. And I'd like to especially acknowledge all the women who came before us, specifically those forced to the margins of society. Their grit, love and curiosity opened every door and window for those who came after.

Text © 2021 Julia De Laurentiis Johnston
Illustrations © 2021 Salini Perera

Published in Canada and the U.S. by Kids Can Press Ltd.
25 Dockside Drive, Toronto, ON M5A 0B5

Kids Can Press is a Corus Entertainment Inc. company

www.kidscanpress.com

The artwork in this book was rendered digitally.
The text is set in Kepler.

Edited by Katie Scott
Designed by Karen Powers

Printed and bound in Malaysia in 10/2020 by Tien Wah Press (Pte.) Ltd.

FSC
www.fsc.org
MIX
Paper from responsible sources
FSC® C012700

CM 21 0 9 8 7 6 5 4 3 2 1

Library and Archives Canada Cataloguing in Publication

Title: Her epic adventure : 25 daring women who inspire a life less ordinary / written by Julia De Laurentiis Johnston ; illustrated by Salini Perera.

Names: De Laurentiis Johnston, Julia, 1982– author. | Perera, Salini, 1986– illustrator.

Description: Includes bibliographical references and index.

Identifiers: Canadiana 20200238469 | ISBN 9781525301100 (hardcover)

Subjects: LCSH: Women adventurers — Biography — Juvenile literature. | LCSH: Adventure and adventurers — Biography — Juvenile literature. | LCSH: Women — Biography — Juvenile literature. | LCGFT: Biographies.

Classification: LCC CT9970 .D45 2020 | DDC j920.72 — dc23

Kids Can Press gratefully acknowledges that the land on which our office is located is the traditional territory of many nations, including the Mississaugas of the Credit, the Anishnabeg, the Chippewa, the Haudenosaunee and the Wendat peoples, and is now home to many diverse First Nations, Inuit and Métis peoples.

We thank the Government of Ontario, through Ontario Creates; the Ontario Arts Council; the Canada Council for the Arts; and the Government of Canada for supporting our publishing activity.